DR PHIL CUMMINS
CHARACTER EDUCATION SERIES

Leading
for Tomorrow's
World

Leading
for Tomorrow's
World

DR PHIL CUMMINS
CHARACTER EDUCATION SERIES

Leading
for Tomorrow's
World

For the architects of my life.

Published in 2025 by Amba Press, Melbourne, Australia
www.ambapress.com.au

© Phil Cummins 2025

All rights reserved. No part of this book may be reproduced or transmitted in any form or by any means, electronic or mechanical, including photocopying, recording or by any information storage and retrieval system, without prior permission in writing from the publisher.

Cover design: Tess McCabe
Internal design: Amba Press
Editor: Rica Dearman

ISBN: 9781923215788 (pbk)
ISBN: 9781923215795 (ebk)

A catalogue record for this book is available from the National Library of Australia.

Contents

Foreword	ix
Introduction: Leading for Tomorrow's World	1

Chapter 1
Service — 3

Service and volunteering	6
Service in your family	9
Service in your friendship groups	12
Service in social clubs and activities	15
Service in sports, the arts and other pursuits	18
Step Forward and Up: Service	22

Chapter 2
Contribution — 27

Disposition towards leadership	31
Becoming a leader	35
Formal leadership	39
Leadership planning and reflection	44
Leadership development	48
Step Forward and Up: Contribution	53
Conclusion: Let's go!	57

Foreword

Hi! My name is Phil.

For more than thirty-five years, as an educator, researcher and speaker, I've been talking with and listening to hundreds of thousands of students, their families and teachers all over the world as they tell me what they want for their lives.

As a parent, grandparent, partner, leader, teacher, writer and thinker, I have learned that the key to living a good and worthwhile life lies in the connection between service and leadership. This means going beyond your wants and desires to put the needs of others ahead of your own. This begins with your family and friends, and it moves beyond as you consider what role you can play in the world as a leader. You can shape this purpose by reflecting on your people and your place. From a deep and sincere respect for others, you can develop your own practice. You'll come to experience the joys of working with others, getting the job done and doing it well as the best version of yourself.

I think there are four ways you can grow in the character, competency and wellness throughout a life of being and becoming the best version of yourself:

1. **A Life of Purpose** – how to identify and claim the fundamental reason why for your journey of exploration, discovery and encounter.

2. **The Pathway to Excellence** – how to learn, live, lead and work as you strive to become the best version of yourself.
3. **Leading for Tomorrow's World** – how to connect your purpose to leadership which influences, inspires, directs and motivates others to build a shared vision for the future.
4. **Make a Difference** – how to create a plan to put your sense of purpose into practice for the sake of people and place and planet.

Drawing on the global research of three organisations that I lead (CIRCLE Education, a School for tomorrow. and the *Game Changers* podcast), I've written four books that explore in turn each of these four ways to grow in character. They're all about helping you to be well and grow in the knowledge, skills, dispositions and habits you need to understand what your purpose is and how you might learn, live, lead and work in pursuit of it.

This book, *Leading for Tomorrow's World*, is about becoming a genuine servant of those around you, a person who co-creates a story of tomorrow that contributes both value and values to the lives of others.

So, what do you want for your life? What's important to you? What will help you to make your mark and measure up? Are you ready to take the big Step Forward and Up in **Leading for Tomorrow's World**?

Let's go!

Phil

Dr Phil Cummins FRSA FACEL FIML
Managing Partner, a School for tomorrow.
Managing Director, CIRCLE – The Centre for Innovation,
  Research, Creativity and Leadership in Education
Associate Professor of Education and Enterprise
Honorary Senior Fellow, University of Melbourne
Host, *Game Changers* podcast

Introduction
Leading for Tomorrow's World

Can you influence a team to build their self-awareness and personal capacity through their learning? Can you inspire people to connect and live with each other and contribute to a shared culture in which we can all grow in character, competency and wellness? Can you direct a team to focus their leadership on serving our community? Can you motivate a team to become the people they need to be and achieve the best outcomes for all through their work?

Leadership is the capacity to influence, inspire, direct and motivate people to achieve their purpose willingly. It is realised through deliberate, targeted and intentional action that aligns vision with intention and means.

Your leadership should begin with who you are as a person, flow into who you want to become and be demonstrated through your actions that respond to the challenge of service with the courage and compassion to meet the expectation to 'go on a journey from me to you to us'. It's about contributing as the leader who changes the game for others as you:

- Strengthen the team through disciplined and purpose-driven practice
- Inform the team by creating and communicating a vision for the future
- Orientate the team to understand and manage change together
- Focus the team on its problem-solving and decision-making
- Align the team to its responsibilities through a values-based leadership style
- Enrich the team by the very act of creating and cultivating the team

To be a game changer, you need to be able to think and rethink about what you do and how you do it. You need to create, just as much as you need to administer. If you are creative and innovative, then not only will you have an understanding of the way that creativity works, but you can also teach it to others. I've learned a few things about the process of creativity that I use in my own work as a writer and leader; I'll share some of these key learnings I have made in my own leadership journey with you as we go.

Leaders need to be able to welcome people of all backgrounds and identities; as they do this work they believe that their distinct perspectives and personal stories will help to make their learning communities more vibrant and creative, and that they will drive both innovation and the hopes of humanity. As such a leader, you can help your people to know that their collective strength comes from their diversity and that in celebrating the visible and invisible qualities of each person, you can ensure that all belong, and are valued and able to reach their inherent possibility.

Are you ready to begin your journey of **Leading for Tomorrow's World**?

Let's go!

Chapter 1
Service

Service

All of us lead in different ways throughout our lives. Leaders do their best work – the building of legacy through the lives of others – when they equip, empower and enable their teams. Leaders build relationships within teams. Leaders help teams to define identities. Leaders help teams to achieve tasks.

The most effective leaders are, therefore, always servant leaders. This means that in their leadership of others, they actively assume responsibility for helping others to be and become people who can grow and contribute towards achieving the mission of the team. They routinely and habitually put others before self. They model selflessness in the example they set.

Chapter 1 is all about this type of service. We will explore five key areas to help you discover how to grow in how and what you learn:

1. Service and volunteering
2. Service in your family
3. Service in your friendship groups
4. Service in social clubs and activities
5. Service in sports, the arts and other pursuits

Let's work through each in turn before you Step Forward and Up and begin to make a plan for your servant leadership.

Service and volunteering

What is service? Do you know how to give of yourself? Are you the servant of your fellows?

The call to lead is, at its core, a call to serve others. This means that we put the interests of others before ourselves and take positive steps to ensure that their needs are met. All of us have the capacity to lead as servants. It does not mean that we are weak and deferential. We must seek to be humble, however, because service requires us to act on an instinct that we are not inherently better or worth more than anyone else. We need to recognise that while different people bring different strengths and weaknesses to any situation, no life is worth more than another.

Our service is how we give of ourselves to others. It comes from our desire to connect with, support and help others to succeed. It goes beyond the simple exchange of self-interest and transactions. We become motivated to transform the lives of others through the habit of kindness, the instinct to serve and the will to give. It is our tangible actions that show how 'us' transcends 'me'. We do need to look after ourselves, but not in a way that causes harm to others, either by our intention or through neglect of their potential to grow and experience progress and wellness.

Context is important because all of us lead in different ways. Some do this on a grand scale, in politics or corporates, while others pursue this in quieter ways through their families and friends. For all, our leadership is the capacity to influence, inspire, direct and motivate others willingly to achieve that which they might not do otherwise – to put the interests and goals of the team or group before their own biologically programmed self-interest. In other words, our service leads others not only to achieve the goal, but to adopt a culture where they support each other through their service. It is compelling and infectious in nature. It is mutual and reciprocal in kind. It starts with the example we set and then calls on us to do what we can to help others, not for our own sake, but because it is good and right to do.

Our servant leadership is, therefore, more than a reflection of our character and competencies. It is also an act of care, of love for others in a particular place. As we lead, we need to continue to encounter others in this place with warmth, openness and generosity of spirit.

Above all, it is the willingness to give that might be described as the essential character of kindness on which our service might be founded. In a perfect world, we would all be perfectly formed with everything we need; we would be complete in and of ourselves. Yet, we know we don't live in such a world. All of us are flawed, all of us are broken, all of us need others. This is why the act of giving is so important.

When we give to others, we shine a light into the dark crevices of their brokenness. At the same time, without this brokenness, the light would be deflected and diffused from an impermeable surface. Without imperfection and vulnerability, we could not share in our humanity. We could not console or bring joy. We could not give. The act of giving, therefore, and the qualities of kindness and service that it embodies, must be located within any process by which we seek to gain in character and lead others. For if we apply the development of character simply to ourselves and the power of leadership only for our own benefit, we miss the point.

The habit of care, the instinct to serve and the will to give must all be learned and incorporated into our character so that they become innate to who we are and how we lead. There are some for whom this seems to flow naturally from their inner being all of their lives. For most of us, however, we need to learn in community how to become less focused on self and more focused on others.

Servant leadership, therefore, is the by-product of a lifelong process of formal and informal education. In time, and through the example and shared expertise of others, we can come to recognise that our leadership should begin with who we are as a person, flow into who we want to become and be demonstrated through our actions in service of others.

For most of us, the refinement of this altruistic intent and its outworking through philanthropic action can only be the result of a deliberate, targeted and planned process of learning the character and competencies of leadership, and service. Accidental transmission of values and attitudes through the chance of the moment is not enough. We all need to understand that there are specific ways to teach and learn about service and giving that are both intentional and spontaneous, explicit and implicit.

Great leaders, mentors and teachers manage to balance all four of these approaches, setting an example of how to give of themselves willingly and voluntarily. Our acts of volunteering, of nominating ourselves to be the ones who will do the work, are important because they demonstrate how to lead as much as their intention to serve reveals the purpose of leadership. This is why 'we teach who we are'; as leaders, it is about both our being and becoming as well as our doing.

We need to learn, therefore, that acting as a servant can be modelled on what we have seen and understood about the device of others. I've learned in my leadership about the importance of the principle of **'iterate or improve'**. I've learned to feel very comfortable not coming up with an idea from scratch, but rather taking somebody else's idea and adapting it to a new context or purpose, or maintaining its current application but improving its impact relative to the outcomes I want to achieve. After all, service isn't really about me. It's much more about you and us.

> ## Reflection: Service and Volunteering
>
> Please consider the following questions:
>
> Am I willing to give up my time to help others?
>
> Am I able to forgive others for their faults and strive to bring joy to their lives in spite of the things that might irritate me about them?
>
> Do I gain a sense of satisfaction from supporting other people to solve their problems?
>
> Am I willing to do the unglamorous and unrecognised work that it takes to get a job done when it needs to be done?
>
> Do I reflect on my service to others and seek to improve what I do to be of the greatest benefit to them?

Service in your family

Do you have healthy habits that serve your family? Are you prepared to respond to their kinship by helping your family members? Do you offer your time, energy and commitment to their progress and wellness?

Family can be complicated. There is much essential value that the experience of family at so many levels gives to so many of us – even if it is an imperfect experience. Most of our popular culture deals with how families are built and work together (or not).

Many families simply don't function well, if at all, and some of us don't have family.

It's not always easy to be kind, to give, to serve – even in one's own family. Yet this is what the wrestling is all about, the journey towards the character of a leader. Family has taught me much in my leadership about the principle of **'complete – never finished'**. From my family, I have gained the permission to treat every solution as an incomplete work in progress that will benefit from further iteration and experimentation to improve its effectiveness and suitability over time. None of us is ever complete as a person, so none of the solutions that we create for each other can ever be final. They're part of a process. They need to be done and completed. But they're never the last step.

The unselfish, unvarnished and ungarnished doing of good things is an act of service that inherently necessitates no response other than gratitude. Service flourishes with mutual acknowledgement and appreciation but can't be the subject of expectation. A kindness done for a kindness may follow in turn, but if it is expected, it may leave both parties in a transactional state of mutual gain, rather than mutual giving. This may benefit both when the going is good but bodes poorly for times when things do not go so well. Deferred gratification for its own sake is also challenging, opening up the provider to the opportunity for manipulation and, in time, even abuse of trust. The need to go on the journey from me to you to us becomes patent – if we don't create a state of 'us', then we must inevitably fall back to self. And family cannot survive when it is motivated primarily by self.

So, for all of the flaws, the quarrels and the variability in the contributions of different members, the shared history of family can be the foundation for learning, living, leading and working in a way that is imbued with the character of giving. Family is, therefore, a likely proving ground for the journey towards the character of a leader. By learning to follow and to lead within family, we can test ourselves in how well we develop the warmth, openness and generosity of spirit that (as we saw earlier) play such a strong role in how we serve and contribute towards others.

These acts of giving, therefore, and the love that they embody, are critical to the reciprocity of servant leadership. If we apply the value of leadership – the giving of our gifts and talents – simply to ourselves, we miss the point. It is family which teaches us this first and, perhaps, for ever.

The giving of kindness to strangers might be awkward, uncomfortable, unreciprocated and uncertain. It might bring us no resolution – and might even be dangerous. But then again, it might not. And that's what makes it so very important. If we didn't have families through which to learn about giving, to acquire selflessness and to practise service, then we would not be able to function as a broader society.

> ### Reflection: Service in your family
>
> Please consider the following questions:
>
> Do I make time in my life to give of myself to my family of my own free will?
>
> Do I help others in my extended family to get along and gain some perspective on things when there is conflict or tension?
>
> Do I strike what is for me the right balance between my obligation and service to my family and my own ambition and goals?

> Do I think a family should have a shared mission and sense of purpose?
>
> Would I contribute my time and leadership to a service or volunteer project that my family would sponsor and run?

Service in your friendship groups

What do you do for your friends? Do you create an environment of support? Do you show them your love for them through who you are and what you do?

Our service towards our friends is an essential component of how we lead. Who we are as people is heavily determined by how we treat those closest to us. Establishing and maintaining constructive service in our friendship groups is a fundamental part of this – how we go about serving our friends and acquaintances through the example we set and the positive and active leadership we provide in the right context.

We might begin by asking ourselves whether we think our friends could count on us to offer the support, and to have genuine, unconditional care for their safety and wellbeing. The answer to this question can largely be found in the history of our behaviour. Our friends should feel these things about us. These are the prerequisites for them knowing that we are dependable, that they can trust us and that, when they need someone, they can call on us.

Our friends represent a significant portion of our support network. They are the people who we can turn to in our darkest moments – we lean on their shoulder to stop us from falling. They fill our days with joy, laughter and memories. They fill our lives with respect, love, enjoyment and kindness. These are things we need to reciprocate.

We never know the impact that simple acts of kindness can have on our friends, be it immediately or in the long term. I know that it can be easy to doubt yourself when you're trying to get this right with your friends. I've learned from my friends about the principle of **'trust the process'**. I've learned that I need to follow my instinct about my own ideas about what might work for them and not worry about their feasibility until the process tells me it is time to test their validity and workability.

We also need to know when to be the friend who says no. We need to be the one who is prepared to make a stand for doing the right thing, the one who gives wise but unpopular counsel at a time when courage is required. It's easy to go with the flow. It's much harder to take responsibility for yourself and for others, especially when doing so can place relationships at risk. True friends support and encourage, inspire and challenge, nurture and protect. They are recognised for what they bring of value to the relationship. Their qualities should not go unnoticed. If these qualities are not recognised, that does not make their exercise any less important.

We also serve our friends in the ways we spend time with them. Sometimes, this is just hanging out and relaxing with no particular purpose in mind. Sometimes, there's more structure to it. Sharing projects and co-curricular activities with our friends is an effective way to build our relationships and provide shared experiences. Sharing the experience of helping or contributing to the lives of others is also an important part of our service.

This support network of friendship shouldn't be exclusive. That's why our service doesn't stop at those who we believe serve us – good leadership, as we keep seeing, goes beyond self-interest. We should be grateful for spaces in which we feel comfortable and loved. We should empathise with those who don't have these. We need to be prepared to be selfless in the welcome we extend to others. We need to invite new people, new friends to share in our spaces, and be kind and welcoming when we do.

Many of our relationships take place at least in part online. We need to be aware that online is not in-person and that virtual relationships can have a particular propensity towards poor behaviour. When we are not face-to-face with our peers, it's easy to forget that our behaviour has consequences. The anonymity and impersonality of the internet can both cloud how we truly feel and also encourage us to show our worst side. It's easy to hide when we are hurt, and it's easier to hide behind our screens when we seek to hurt others. We need to be kind, we need to be cautious and we need to reserve intimacy of any type for those with whom we share a physical space. Part of our service to our friends involves the way we model honourable behaviours that put our values into action online and how we seek to actively influence the culture of our friends to do the right thing.

Encouraging our friends to support and give back to the community is one of the responsibilities we have as a leader in our friendship groups. As we hope to go on a journey to seek purpose through service, we should encourage those closest to us to join us.

> ### Reflection: Service in your Friendship Groups
>
> Please consider the following questions:
>
> Can my friends count on me to offer support and to watch out for our safety and wellbeing?

Is my friendship group diverse in its composition and does this encourage me to be more open in my outlook?

Will my friends and I invite outsiders to join in our activities?

Do I use social media in a way that does not demean, harm or isolate others, and will I stand up if I see that happening?

Do my friends and I often volunteer together to support an activity or project that helps others?

Service in social clubs and activities

Do you have a practical approach to providing service in social activities and clubs? Do you manage how you volunteer your time and other resources to support their ongoing viability? Do you help those in the communities of your social activities and clubs to feel as though they belong?

The communities of the social activities and clubs to which we belong allow us to engage in activities that are enjoyable and important for our development. The least we can do in return for our sense of belonging within them and all the wonderful experiences we've had as a result is to support their continuity, growth and change. Serving our clubs and social communities allows us to reciprocate in kind for what others have given to us. When we, along with our peers, commit to this attitude, our communities and clubs will begin to grow. This shared culture will mean more enjoyment and fulfilment for everyone.

Organising, managing and running activities and events within our clubs and communities is a clear way we can serve them and the people within them. What we are doing through this is engineering new opportunities for the healthy parts of our communities and clubs to come to life. We can help people to connect; we can encourage new members to join; we can work towards growth in the breadth and depth of togetherness in our community.

Doing what we can to make our community or club accessible and welcoming is another area of our service towards it. Being kind and demonstrating an interest in the activity and desire of others to be involved helps others to feel comfortable as part of the group. We should be welcoming and make new participants feel secure in their place and supported in their growth. We should avoid being cliquey and exclusive.

From our own service in a community, we can bring to it an understanding of how to sponsor a philosophy and a practice of service in others. This begins with the roles we play. Striving to be a contributor as a servant in a social club or activity is about identifying the unmet needs or challenges faced by members of this community. It's about providing innovative, creative and sustainable solutions to them. My leadership learning through my own involvement in service to social activities and clubs has taught me the importance of the principle of **'test, tinker, trash'**. In the roles I have played, I have been encouraged to try out different prototypes, models and hypotheses, recording my findings and observations as I go, before implementing in scale only those things that work. You can apply this same approach in order to spread a shared practice of service that will become ingrained in the culture of the community.

Taking part in service projects or initiatives through a community can further the impact on the lives of others. This first-hand experience of the effect of service helps to inspire more selflessness.

It also promotes the willingness of people to act as role models, those whose philanthropic purpose, activity and courage enables them to contribute to and improve the lives of others.

Contributing as a good member is not always something that presents itself to us obviously. We need to track down these opportunities, armed with the intention to serve others. These are times when we should put in the effort to be an active listener, and for us to step forward when we see someone in our community without someone to talk to. We know what the right thing to do is. We know how to serve. We know when to serve. We just have to do it.

> ### Reflection: Service in Social Clubs and Activities
>
> Please consider the following questions:
>
> Am I currently involved in service projects or initiatives through my school or community agencies?
>
> Do I admire and follow those philanthropists who identify a big problem or challenge and leverage significant change and betterment?
>
> Have I helped to manage and run a club or other activity recently?
>
> Do I try to make sure that my involvement in an activity or club is inclusive and respectful of all?
>
> Am I a willing and helpful volunteer when I hear the call to contribute to make something successful?

Service in sports, the arts and other pursuits

Do you know how to locate your capacity to contribute your service in sports, the arts and other pursuits within a framework of your values? Do you build respect within them? Do you know how to balance competition and enjoyment?

We are blessed to have sports, the arts and other pursuits that we enjoy and make us feel fulfilled. They represent opportunities for our lives to become richer through the acquisition of skills and team relationships, the experience of community and exposure to the creative pieces of our humanity.

Teams and the pastimes we share with others often form the basis of the communities to which we belong. These communities require all members to actively support, and to feel actively supported by the team. Our teammates and peers in our hobbies are people we should actively care for and support. As always, our leadership and service extend to building a culture. Establishing a sense of respect, purpose, humility, determination, success and community through our words and actions supports everybody sharing the space with us. It creates a sense of togetherness that allows us to become an aligned team or unit in which we all understand our roles, the collective ambition and the necessity of our commitment to each other.

This is further supported when a team is committed to service, rather than any one individual. This is when our selflessness and dedication can come to the fore.

This requires a high level of respect. Respect is earned every day and accrues because of the relative quality of what we do and the weight of its contribution to the cause of the team. It does come automatically. Respect means appreciating the strengths and contributions of team members just as much as it means deploying our competencies to play our part. Respect means supporting our teammates through good times and bad. In particular, it means helping those who are having a hard time and trusting that they will do the same for us.

Respect, however, does not mean blind support. There will be times when we will need to criticise, when we will need to stand up to others, and also times when we will need to protect others. Coming to the defence of our teammates demonstrates to them that they are cared for by their team and their community. It shows the character that says everyone deserves kindness and a loyal friend in their corner.

There will be times when members of our teams will disagree with us. Conflict is natural and it can be especially common in areas like sports and the arts when an individual's performance and sense of self-importance can have a heightened influence over team culture or community dynamics and perception of them. This inevitably means that there will be times when we are frustrated, argue and disagree about the best way to do things. In these moments, our service is demonstrated by our capacity to resolve conflict, bring people together and solve problems.

This involves the ability to take a step back, think through the problem at hand, and locate the causes and address them together. I've found my leadership involvement in sports, the arts and other pursuits to be a really crucial lesson in the importance of not necessarily running with the first idea that pops into my head. This is the principle of **'come back later'**. I have learned from my involvement in teams, orchestras, bands and choirs about the value of being able to leave an idea or thought half-formed and pick it up again later when time and resources allow me to bring it to fruition more successfully.

Yet, even then, things don't always go right. It is important that the efforts of our teammates are not blamed or subject to an unnecessarily critical analysis of what has already occurred. What is much more constructive is the recognition of the outcome as a by-product of circumstance and the forging of a commitment to fixing the situation for the better of all next time. Nonetheless, if we see something that is unacceptable according to the values of the team, we should be prepared to identify it and make it clear that this is not 'the way we do things here'.

Throughout history, there have been teams of people in sports and the arts who succeeded not because of individual brilliance, but because of the whole team's commitment to a shared set of values and a vision for who they might become. Through our service, we can all help create this shared vision and the success that can flow from it. It also helps if we have a commitment to winning or winning through together, and doing so in such a way, we can all feel as though we have done so with honour.

A result or a performance becomes a win when it helps us to feel as though we belong, it helps us to grow, and it is done in pursuit of something which is good and right. It becomes about 'us' and our growth. When we lose or when we don't hit the required mark, we can console each other and look for further growth next time. Competition hones the performance of any teams but should be viewed with perspective. No win is worth sacrificing the culture of the team. When we look back and remember what we did together, we will tell stories about both wins and losses, about good days and bad days. Most of all, we will be remembered for the character we added to the team and our capacity to bring benefits from our service to others.

Reflection: Service in Sports, the Arts and Other Pursuits

Please consider the following questions:

Will I help name the problem and address it if the team or group cohesion is not going well?

Will I reach out to a teammate or member of an activity who seems to be struggling?

Am I always prepared to speak up if I think someone is being demeaned or harassed?

Are the values and ethos of the team or activity just as important to me as its success?

Do I believe that every team should have a service initiative or project attached to it?

Step Forward and Up
Service

Based on everything you have thought about over the course of this chapter, it's time for you to build a plan to Step Forward and Up in your service. We are going to use the Plus, Minus, Interesting process first developed by Dr Edward de Bono, and it's important for you to write down your answers to each of these:

- **Plus** – What's one idea from this chapter that you could make happen in your life tomorrow? What could you do to make this happen? What help will you need? What's a really practical first thing that you could do to make this idea real in your life? What will you do to keep going? How will you know when it's making a difference?

- **Minus** – What's one idea from this chapter that doesn't seem right for you? Why isn't this idea right for you? Is it a case of 'not at all' or 'not yet'? How do you know whether you should hold your ground or shift your thinking on this idea?

- **Interesting** – What's one idea from this chapter that seems like it might be an interesting thing to do but which you're not yet ready to embrace? What might you need to do to ready yourself for this challenge? Who or what might help you to prepare you to take up this challenge in due course? How will you allow the time and space to do this preparation?

It can be hard to take a positive action to make changes that you think will help you to grow and change in how you lead others. So much of this comes down to what you are prepared to give of yourself in the process.

Sacred scriptures around the world teach us the golden rule to 'do unto others as we would have done to ourselves'. Even if you're not religious, principles of humanism will teach you that humans cannot simply do and act as they please. Each of us needs to act in accordance with principles that recognise the need for reciprocity or, as Africans might express it, '*Ubuntu* – I am because you are'. That's the basis for any healthy and functioning community: mutual acts of service that we give to each other.

So, whether you are coming from a faith basis or whether your values and beliefs are grounded in secular humanism, you will need to align both the habits and instincts of service to what it is that you do as a leader. Many approaches to leadership work on the exterior first: skills, capabilities, competencies. Yet doing this is a bit like working on a house – we can paint the exterior any way we like, but without solid construction and a fitting place within its surroundings, no amount of surface modification can make up for poor architecture. In the same way, we cannot 'make' leaders anything other than who they are. They must lead from the core of their being and express their service as a by-product of this character.

Our service as leaders, therefore, is realised through what we give of ourselves to others. It is the articulation of a desire to achieve better outcomes for all. We develop this as we pursue what I call **The Pathway to Excellence**, an inside-out process of development that models growth through the asking and answering of these four questions:

- ✓ Self-awareness: Who am I?
- ✓ Relationship: Where do I fit in?
- ✓ Selflessness: How can I best serve others?
- ✓ Vocation: Whose am I?

The second book in this series explores **The Pathway to Excellence** in much greater detail. But it's important to realise that leadership is learned and revealed from the inside-out; it's about how you can integrate your service to others within your own journey of becoming the best version of yourself. That's why it's so relevant in this context.

The sooner you realise that the inside-out process of asking and answering these four key questions lies more tangibly in your selflessness and your calling to serve, then the more likely it is that you will commit yourself not to the self-centred and ultimately self-defeating pursuit of a pathway to perfection (which is really about satisfying yourself by trying to achieve the impossible), but rather to a pathway to excellence (which, while it can never be fully realised and is therefore always imperfect, is much more likely to result in the satisfaction of the needs of others as well as yourself). The creation of a sense of belonging, the fulfilment of potential and the doing of good and right through your leadership, therefore, invokes both an awareness of the other and the self.

There is a corresponding scope and sequence for the developmental milestones along the journey: self-awareness, relationship, selflessness and vocation. This is, therefore, a critical factor in helping to answer the question 'who am I?' Self-awareness is not simply a solipsistic exercise; it is always truly grounded in location to the situation of others – relationship, the choice to place their needs before one's own – selflessness, and the development of a sense of purpose that goes beyond the simple acquisition of resources and becomes a genuine consideration of how one might act to better the condition of all – vocation.

Growing in these four capacities allows us to complete the asking and answering of the questions on the four steps of **The Pathway to Excellence** as a leader by asking what it is that you might give.

Giving in to the need to learn and grow allows you to come to know yourself by asking 'who am I?' Giving your gifts and talents allows you to earn your place by asking 'where do I fit in?' Giving to the journey 'from me to you to us' allows you to ask 'how can I best serve others?' Giving up selfish control of others in favour of selfless service allows both you and them to take full responsibility for your progress and find your calling by asking 'whose am I?'

What might you do to give more or to give more wholly of yourself through cultivating your:

- ✓ Service and volunteering?
- ✓ Service in your family?
- ✓ Service in your friendship groups?
- ✓ Service in social clubs and activities?
- ✓ Service in sports, the arts and other pursuits?

What would you need to leave behind to enable you to do this?

Whose help will you need to help you make this happen?

Take your time to think about how these changes in who you are and who you are becoming might work out in your daily life. When you are ready, let's start Chapter 2, so we can explore the second element of your leadership: contribution.

Let's go!

Chapter 2
Contribution

Contribution

As you grow in your leadership, you will learn to turn purpose into practice through the contributions you make to your key relationships and to society. You will lead by example and actively encourage others to develop positively as individuals within your community towards achieving the organisation's aspirations – its vision and goals. At the same time, effective leaders also help bring about change and look after people on this journey.

To do all of this well, you will need to demonstrate resilience, persistence, initiative and a high level of connectedness to your organisation, team and its members. As you grow in your leadership, you will most likely experience some progress, achievement and success on a personal, team, organisational and societal level.

This chapter focuses on the contributions you can make as a leader and how to boost your capacity to make these contributions. We will explore five key areas to help you discover how to grow in how and what you learn:

1. Disposition towards leadership
2. Becoming a leader
3. Formal leadership
4. Leadership planning and reflection
5. Leadership development

Let's work through each in turn before you Step Forward and Up and strengthen your leadership plan with a strong appreciation of the contributions that you can give.

Disposition towards leadership

Do you know how to build and direct your disposition towards leadership? Do you make specific choices about what you will and will not do to lead? Do you maintain a positive approach towards taking responsibility for leading others?

I'd like to encourage you to reflect on the need to cultivate a disposition for leadership. It's about having a positive attitude towards service and contribution that values the dignity, worth and contributions of others, that shows respect for people, culture and place, and that wants to deliver the results that a team, organisation or community wants and expects. It's about driving our learning, growth and potential to thrive in tomorrow's world.

Who could have imagined the remarkable changes of our times? The pace of life, the ever-increasing sense of connectedness with all parts of the globe and our increasing respect for the contributions of so many communities make it impossible to shut out the rest of the world. Indeed, we are a vital part of this world, one which increasingly causes us to adapt what we do, and therefore who we are, to thrive as valuable and valued servants and contributors.

Many people around the world now have a much greater appreciation of the value of a person, especially in terms of the need to protect the freedoms of the individual and the imperative for us to respect difference in individuals. The same applies for the groups and communities which comprise our society.

Once, it was considered normal (and even desirable) to give a hard time to newcomers or those whose lives did not match those of the mainstream. Now, it is (we trust) not the 'done' thing.

Some, however, yearn for what they imagine was a simpler past. They struggle to see beyond the confines of their prejudices. Others embrace a cosmopolitan world view. Neither of these groups is necessarily better than the other; all contribute, sometimes with glory and sometimes with shame, to our human condition.

It is this very human condition, with all of its attendant strengths and frailties, which informs our sense of what it means to be all of one. The tensions between the individual and the group, the powerful and the powerless, the idealistic and the pragmatic, the conformists and the rebellious have always been a part of human existence. That we aspire to a more coherent society will not make these competing tensions go away.

Sometimes, making sense of the world is not such an easy thing to do. I have learned in my own leadership about the importance of the principle of clearing my mind and my diary so that I can **'wander and wonder'**. I need to feel as though I can explore possibilities and ask questions about what might come next and what might be different without any negative reaction or threat of adverse consequence. I've learned to have faith in my capacity to think things through without the weight of the world on my shoulders.

In the same way, we should have confidence in each other and our potential. Therefore, we should help others to try new opportunities, and we should also expect them to be taken. We should want people to be intellectually curious, responsive, persistent and enriched by the possibilities. We should want them to recognise and honour the privileges which have been given to them, to become compassionate citizens of the world, and to seek wisdom and knowledge through trust, fidelity, friendship and faith.

I believe it is an essential characteristic of our contemporary world that inclusive and open thinking, which seeks to serve the common good, should be a strong part of the traditions of a community, its leadership and its culture. We should enshrine the belief that all people have intrinsic value both to give and receive support from the community.

At the heart of an inclusive philosophy is the fundamental point of view that one person's wellbeing cannot be gained at the expense of the 'other'. It is important that we all are conscious of the necessity to help those in special need to achieve their goals, encourage the establishment of a compassionate and empathetic community that is inclusive and respects diversity, and sees itself as a catalyst for inclusivity – supporting and empowering people. It is important for us to recognise that a caring community does not simply emerge as a by-product of good intentions. It presents a goal that has to be deliberately planned and worked towards – it must be the outcome of the good leadership of all of us.

This should not weaken our determination to make our lives and the lives of all better. This is our truth for the 21st century – we can resolve this challenging set of competing interests by enhancing the dignity of all those involved in our adventure. In doing this, it is far more constructive for us to start with recognising and celebrating what we are good at, and then move on from there to more difficult ground. It is in this way that we are likely to build and lead together, and to develop a greater understanding of all of those who make up our society.

Our mandate to lead should be directed foremost by what is best for our communities, as opposed to that which will promote our own interests and fuel our ambitions for power, prestige or material gain. In seeking to exercise an agency which is based on sharing and optimising the contributions of all towards the preferred future, however, we must be careful to avoid:

- The tyranny of niceness – the tendency towards an easy likability that prevents the sharing of pure thought and unfiltered truth when it is needed.
- The tyranny of self-deprecation – the false modesty that prevents the sharing of our gifts of effective leadership.

- The tyranny of harmony – the avoidance of constructive conflict that prevents the sharing of boldness, risk-taking and innovation inherent in bringing about meaningful and positive change.

Leadership, therefore, starts with a disposition to serve and to contribute. This arises from the values we choose to help ground us in an understanding of who we are and what our purpose might become. They flow from us to our actions and then into a desire to contribute, to make a difference for the better in the lives of others, a desire to help others and to want to put their needs before our own.

Reflection: Disposition towards Leadership

Please consider the following questions:

Do I believe that leadership is not something innate but rather a competency that can be learned over time?

Am I strongly motivated to become a leader who has a wide array of relevant knowledge, skills, dispositions and learning habits?

Am I passionate about becoming a servant leader who helps others to thrive and contribute their best effort to the work at hand?

Do I find and value the time to reflect on and deepen my sense of purpose at the heart of my leadership?

Do I take full advantage of opportunities to reflect on and learn from the different leadership perspectives and styles I observe and witness around me?

Becoming a leader

Do you recognise your potential to be a leader? Can you overcome your hesitations and doubts about yourself? Are you willing to take a big step forward and up to take on the challenge to serve and contribute?

People unwilling to learn and grow will never achieve their potential. You have a responsibility as a leader to create teams and groups that share this passion for rigorous learning. To do this, you need to set clear and high expectations for all team members, promote depth over breadth and stimulate integration of new ideas into a tangible and even joyful experience of a better life together.

When we step into the role of a leader, people can often view us with some unease or even hostility to begin with. The entry of a new person into a new role will have an impact on their lives and their uncertainty about this may affect how they see us to begin with. We may need to earn their respect before they will give us their respect.

This is normal. We should not walk into a position and assume that it carries any special status other than the privilege to serve in a particular capacity.

People will rely on us, and we need to show what we are made of before we can reasonably expect them to align themselves with our values and what we want them to do for and with us. They will, almost certainly, want to be involved in some capacity with decision-making, but they will expect that we will bear the risk and responsibility of the ultimate decisions. They may question everything until experience proves to them that what is being done is right. Then, over time, they may come to support the vision that you have built with them and what is asked of them so strongly that, in due course, we may ask them to consider anew what needs to be done as circumstances – and, therefore, both the goals and the operational processes relating to them – will change.

As leaders, we need to balance this drive towards the achievement of a vision with the creation of a shared story of trust and hope. This principle of **'tell the story'** is one of the most important lessons I have learned as a leader. In any leadership context, I must find my own voice, agency and advocacy and use it to co-create with others a narrative of the journey of exploration, encounter and discovery which we pass on to others.

Bringing people, resources, vision and goals together to climb a mountain that we may not have climbed before can be exhilarating and, at the same time, frustrating. Trust is an essential component of this. So much of the pursuit of excellence, the gaining of success and the celebration of victory is based on the understanding that others have 'got your back'. Trust can take years to build and seconds to destroy. We must nurture it carefully and consistently.

In a similar fashion, hope plays such an important and motivating role in our lives. As long as we have hope, a positive future is there for us to attain. That is why leadership always has a future orientation. In many respects, leadership is about clarifying vision and holding out hope to those who are responsible for making it happen on the ground. Hope is also a reflection of the strength of our faith: faith in ourselves, faith in those around us, faith in our values, faith in our purpose.

The opposite of hope, of course, is despair. Normally our goals are what inspire us, but not when we think they are impossible. If we lose all hope, we will never know whether we could have succeeded. Leaders fight fear regularly. Occasionally, it gets the better of us and we become overly circumspect and start playing things safe.

Faith, hope, love, injustice – these higher goals remind leaders that this is the only leadership life we get. But what type of person do you need to become to lead and to live this life?

There is no call here for the selfish achievement of one's own ends at the expense of others. Instead, there is a call to join in a community and share your passion for high standards in a way that adds to the culture of your organisation. In this way, we can see that while all of us have our part to play in helping each other become excellent in all that we attempt, the true passion of a leader is for the growth of the team, the development of the individuals in it and the achievement of the team's mission and goals.

Building passion for and in the team means you feel inspired to do what you want to do, you see the value in pursuing this dream, and you can locate and commit the energy to make this happen. In this way, your passion as a leader becomes your purpose, and your purpose becomes your passion.

We need to be noticed for our willingness to make hard decisions with compassion and an understanding that clarity is a very specific act of kindness. None of us can grow when the direction we are given is vague and the feedback lacks honesty. This does not mean we should be cruel or untactful. There are ways of delivering challenging feedback and bad news which preserve the dignity and worth of individuals and whole teams. We can learn how to do these without resorting to sandwiching difficult ideas between two pieces of praise. People will learn very quickly to wait for the 'but', so positive feedback should be kept well clear of challenging conversation.

We also need to be promoters of innovation and renewal. We may not come up with many, or indeed any, of the great ideas ourselves, but we need to be champions of those who do and establish processes that help new ideas to be tested and find homes in which, over time, they might flourish.

As we seek to realise the vision together, we also need to be willing to adapt to the circumstances. We need a range of practical leadership styles that speak to the context of the moment as much as they do the more enduring culture of the organisation. We need to align our values and how they are enacted through the mission of our role with the ethos and strategy of our organisation. We need to model and explain this to our team and help them to do the same.

Enthusiasm for the work is essential, as is calmness in a crisis. No one will ever pay us to lose our tempers or to go off on flights of fancy without having thought things through at least in outline form. At the same time, we need to help people to organise their work and demonstrate to them what is expected of them and when it needs to be done.

Above all, we need to understand the 'why', the compelling rationale for the work and how the work of the team will fit together to achieve the task. It is a professional courtesy to invite team members to contribute to the 'what' of the role, the details of how they might go about getting a task done and the goals they will set to do this. Our encouragement and patience will go a long way to helping them to build routines and habits that create order, predictability and incremental improvement in their work over time.

Reflection: Becoming a Leader

Please consider the following questions:

Do I believe that I have a valuable role to play as a leader?

> Do I research opportunities to learn more about leadership?
>
> Am I willing to show the curiosity, compassion, courage and conviction to step into leadership?
>
> Am I prepared to put the needs of others before myself in making a selfless contribution as a leader?
>
> Do I feel an obligation to become a steward of and an ambassador for the organisations and institutions to which I belong?

Formal leadership

Do you want to take up a formal position of leadership? Are you willing to put in the work to be successful with this? Are you willing to acquire the character needed to lead well?

We have seen already in this book that leadership is about the art of influencing, inspiring, directing and motivating people so that they work together to achieve the goals of the team or the broader organisation. Often, we will show leadership qualities by supporting the formal leadership of others and by doing what we do as well as we can as a service for others. Most of us, however, will be presented with opportunities to exhibit leadership in formal positions infused with authority to take action and make decisions to build the future together.

We need to choose where and how we want to lead, and ensure that the scope and sequence of these are realistic. We need to be brave in applying for roles while remaining open to the possibilities that call us to a position of formal leadership. The advice and support of those around us are essential.

Understanding who you are as a leader is as much about defining your sense of purpose as anything else. For it is through our sense of mission that we are most formed in terms of our leadership practice. Our beliefs about what is important drive our narrative, the reason why we do what we do. Our leadership task in this respect is to convince those around us of the worthiness of this purpose. In doing so, our leadership becomes an opportunity to shape and enhance our present and future culture in our changing world through the application of an honourable purpose.

Our formal leadership and its purpose arises from, and is expressed through, our character. Character is about the mark and measure of people who seek to attain a sense of belonging through their civic character, reach their potential by enhancing their performance character, and develop a set of fundamental beliefs about what is good and right by forming their moral character.

As leaders, we need to grow in this character and help others to become people who can also influence, inspire, direct and motivate others to achieve a common purpose. The foundation of this is our capacity to help them to grow in character and demonstrate this through:

- The integrity to lead a meaningful life as a good person – this draws on the skill of self-management, which is about building personal organisation, resilience, adaptability, self-awareness, response to feedback and personal responsibility.
- The ability to manage complexity with authenticity as a future builder – this draws principally on the skill of communication, which is about building influence, understanding of others, relationships, connection with audiences, numeracy and the capacity to listen, speak and write.

- The capacity to grow and transform as a continuous learner and unlearner – the skill of learning through technology is critical in this respect, especially through engagement in learning, developing new capabilities, supporting others to learn and the building of digital fluency, digital citizenship and management of data.
- The wisdom to provide sustainable direction to the world as a solution architect with the skill of problem solving that is shown through evaluation, decision-making, creativity and innovation, reasoning, consultations with stakeholders and the generation of options.
- The perspective to balance the local, regional and global selflessly as a responsible citizen with the skill of planning and organising through capacity in initiative, taking action, managing risk, managing resources, implementation and review.
- The willingness to work well in relationship with others to bring success and fulfilment for all as a team creator with the skill of teamwork that comprises collaboration, cooperation, respect, ethical conduct, team wellbeing and professional culture.

To do this, we strengthen through disciplined and purpose-driven practice, and we inform through creating and communicating vision. We orientate through understanding and managing change, and we focus through problem-solving and decision-making. We align through a values-based leadership style, and we enrich through team cultivation.

We should, to the best of our ability, and given the context of our experiences and personal situation, want to grow stronger in the exercise of these capabilities of game-changing leadership throughout our lives. Great communities need to build on a strong core of leaders with these capabilities, who really care and have ideas, and the moral will to persist. What is needed for sustainable long-term performance and improvement is leadership at many levels of the organisation.

Our leadership, then, is not simply a role or an assigned position; it is earned and affirmed by those with whom we work. Every day, our community members model leadership to and inspire each other. And so, leadership is a way of being in the community, a way of being among friends, a way of taking on challenges, and most centrally, a way of building capacity and vision through purpose and culture in the ones we are called to serve and to bring honour to the institution and its people.

How we do this, however, is not necessarily predictable. One lesson I have learned is about the principle of **'evolve and capture'**. I need to be allowed initially to sketch out a simple concept, then work to a loose timeline to make it real with minimal requirements for paperwork, drawing up solutions in detail only when I know that they work and are ready to be shared.

We can also consider a multidimensional model for the exercise of our leadership capabilities that is both purposeful and relational in nature as to what we do in different circumstances and reflect on how we can improve their performance holistically through this approach:

- **Personal leadership:** We need to consider how leaders build relationships with individuals. This is the fundamental toolkit of the team leader who directs and motivates. For organisational leaders, it can be more effective for the majority of individual relationships to be built on their ability to inspire and influence through opportunities for providing aspiration and engagement. While many might wish to spend more time here, the reality is that the greater the responsibility, the more limited their capacity becomes to create meaningful and sustainable deep relationships as they might have when they practised their craft earlier in their careers.

- **Tactical leadership:** We need to create teams and build relationships within them that enable us to get the job done well. In many ways, we have more opportunity to interact with a greater number of teams, but in doing so, we can probably only allow ourselves so much time to spend with them before we need to move on to another group. As such, our role is to enhance the journey of the team through the commitment of energy and emotion combined with role-modelling.
- **Strategic leadership:** We need to apply ourselves to helping solve the strategic challenges of our wider organisation. Again, we need to make wise choices as to how we invest our time by focusing on the things that will make the greatest difference in the long run. We need to create a vision to help the organisation align, implement and evaluate what it does to ensure the greatest positive impact on intention, design and culture.
- **Global leadership:** We also need to connect our organisation with its wider world. In this respect, we are building a relationship with the organisation's different and intersecting communities, negotiating and advocating for the place of the school and the value proposition of what it offers. In doing so, we assist the organisation to define its preferred position and to situate itself within its context by reinforcing its purpose, commitment and connections within the community.

Reflection: Formal leadership

Please consider the following questions:

Do I believe that each of us has a responsibility to help our communities and its members to thrive?

> Do I aspire, in time, to hold positions of formal leadership?
>
> Do I engage in a wide variety of community, educational and/or work-related activities in which I can learn about how to lead in a practical setting?
>
> Am I learning about how to adapt my leadership to different situations and the people within them?
>
> Do I have a clear sense of my purpose as a leader and how to bring values and value to the lives of others?

Leadership planning and reflection

Have you adopted healthy habits of planning and reflecting on your leadership? Do you make and take opportunities to reflect on your capacity to lead? Do you evaluate your leadership and the potential for learning through different leadership experiences?

There's an old Yiddish proverb my grandmother used to use: *Der Mensch Tracht und Gott Lacht*, which translates as 'Man Plans and God Laughs'. It is challenging to set and realise plans because there is so much that falls out of our control. Try as we might to impose an order on things and circumstances can change the course of events just when we think we are getting on top of things.

Nonetheless, if we are going to make a positive difference through our service as leaders, we need to take the time to review what we are doing in our roles and the impact this is having on those around us. We then need to take responsibility to anticipate as best we can the type of personal and professional development that might help us to be the best leader that we can be.

It begins with an understanding that we need to develop an intention to lead that is driven by the desire to serve. People will need to know what we have to offer and why they might want to follow us. We need more than good character. We need to have a clear idea about where we might go together and what it will take for us to get there. Mentors and advisors are very helpful in gaining insight into our leadership, yet, as with all character apprenticeship relationships, we need to learn when to step away and exercise our emerging expertise ourselves.

We need to do our own work by ourselves at times. This principle of **'leave me alone'** is a valuable lesson I have learned in my leadership. I regularly need freedom from distraction and interruption so that I can prepare myself, focus on my own thoughts, and generate ideas that could prove to be of interest and relevance.

We need to continue to learn and read about leadership. While a wide range of experience in informal leadership situations is helpful for us to rehearse our competencies, there is nothing that can take the place of creating vision, building a team, solving problems and making decisions in real time. It is here that leadership is really tested: do we do this thing or not? If so, how will we do it? When will we know whether it is successful? What happens when something goes wrong? What happens when we achieve our goals? These are questions which we need to train a team to work through together, a team that will crave authentic and insightful leadership to help it do what it needs to do, especially in forming and driving forward a sense of the mission, the steps that need to be taken to achieve it and the roles, responsibilities and resources required to make it happen.

This is why we need to establish a portfolio of responsibilities in experiences of leadership to which we are formally appointed, and plan the way in which we will go about moving from position to position. This is not for the sake of personal ambition, but so that we can develop the corresponding portfolio of knowledge, skills, dispositions and learning habits that will allow us to move forward with more success.

The most important of these will be the habits of regular review and reflection that we build into our daily, weekly, monthly and annual calendars. We need to take a proactive approach to eliciting feedback from all of those around us as to how we are performing our role and what we might need to do to improve. Then we can improve the performance of the team and its capacity not only to achieve its mission, but also support the individual and group needs of team members.

Leadership is not simply a popularity contest; there is hard and sometimes unpleasant work to be done along the way, and wise leaders know how to support and motivate. We need to learn how to encourage and direct people. We need to know when to praise and when to correct faults. We need to know when to move forward, when to pause and when to withdraw from situations so that we regroup and try a different approach. We need to understand how to manage progress by stages, including how to build processes of research and testing into what we do together so that we do not simply commit huge amounts of resources, energy and human capital for their own sake.

We need to go beyond simply leading by example and create a personal model for leadership based on the values to which we hold most closely. We need to use the central concepts of this model as the pillars through which we will organise our thinking, reflection and planning about leadership, the questions we ask of ourselves and our impact, and the approach we will take in leading others. These concepts need not be exhaustive, but they must speak to what is important to us and the context in which we operate. We also need to be prepared to change this model when, as will inevitably be the case, our circumstances change over time. As what is real and what is meaningful in our context changes, so must we adapt how we identify and create the structures that define our leadership.

> ### Reflection: Leadership planning and reflection
>
> Please consider the following questions:
>
> Do I have a clear but flexible plan to improve my leadership across my responsibilities and aspirations in a variety of settings?
>
> Do I reflect constantly on the quality of my work as a leader, using a variety of sources of feedback and information to help me get better?
>
> Do I have a track record for commitment, reliability, initiative and self-discipline that is fundamental to my reputation in all the settings in which I contribute and lead?
>
> Do I take a holistic and integrated perspective on my leadership in many settings, centred by my sense of purpose, integrity and the values that matter most to me?
>
> Is the first goal of my leadership development planning to ensure that I am developing my perspective and competencies as a 21st-century leader?

Leadership development

Do you want to learn how to be a better leader? Do you know what excellence and greatness in leadership look like? What sort of legacy do you want to leave as a leader?

Leadership development is the process by which we gain increasing competency in how we lead. This learning can be exercised in different formal and informal contexts and is best executed through a deliberate, targeted and intentional fashion; accidental leadership is a poor primary means of acquiring competency for those who are serious about taking responsibility for their community. Accepting the call to leadership is a commitment to a lifetime of studying how best to create teams that achieve better outcomes for all, and perhaps even greatness.

Greatness in leadership begins with understanding excellence. Something which is excellent is of the highest quality, the consequence of the highest level of performance; it exceeds normal expectations and through its virtue and worth becomes exemplary. It sets the standard to be followed.

I believe that excellence is best achieved through leadership in which we actively assume responsibility for serving others in order to achieve the mission of the team. We need to lead by example and encourage other team members to develop positively as individuals within our community towards achieving our aspirations – our vision and goals.

The most meaningful and consistent measure of excellence is by considering its impact – the lives and communities it changes for the better. The accomplishments of individuals and teams who have made a meaningful difference serve to inspire others by their achievements to pursue even greater heights of excellence as a community.

Excellence does not stop with attaining a personal best – it is an ongoing process and one which must involve and engage with those around us. It is, therefore, all about others and the teams who serve them. We should strive to embrace the concept of excellence and pursue it with a combination of humility and willpower to enhance the dignity of all.

We need to develop a sound understanding of the traditions and practices of our community and represent the interests of all members. We should aim to reinforce our community's expectations in relation to tone and discipline. To achieve this, we acknowledge the need to demonstrate resilience, persistence, initiative and a high level of connectedness to the team, its members and its culture.

We also need to learn everything we can to develop in our leadership. This principle to **'do your homework'** is a critical lesson I have learned. I have a strong need to learn everything I can about the field in which I seek to lead so that I am approaching it with clear knowledge and understanding about what has come before and be well placed to think about what might come next.

Part of this involves being willing to do this homework over and over so that I become better at what I do. I believe that to become great, we need to begin by doing our best and then do it even better time and time again. It means trying to be excellent and also achieving the standards required. These standards must start high and be achievable, and then, when attained, they must be raised higher still.

This implies two things. First, our understanding of 'our best' must grow and improve over time. Second, we must accept that we are unlikely to be great in our leadership all of the time. As the days rush by, we can become aware that there is so much more that we hope to achieve, more people that we need to meet, and more that we need to say and do. Nevertheless, the path is clearly before us, and we must be confident that we are in the company of many good companions. This can be daunting at times, but we cannot stand still while our lives unfold around us – we need to live in the moment, relishing every opportunity that comes our way. After all, what life are we waiting for?

Maturity involves a constant struggle with personal integrity. It is a journey, a pilgrimage, rather than a static point of being. This struggle is a creative enterprise and ceasing to struggle leads to disintegration. We begin our struggle for excellence by following. There are no 'born leaders'. We start by following our parents, our siblings, and older children at school and in our community. Later, we follow teachers, coaches, managers and mentors. Eventually, writers and historic figures enter our lives as leaders, and we follow them. And then somewhere along the line, whether we realise it or not, people start following us. We become leaders – all of us.

Leadership development is, therefore, an ongoing process. When we step into this process, we need to aim to be the very best we can be at leading and learning within a discourse that is built on asking and answering questions. Rather than predetermining people as 'leaders' or 'non-leaders', we believe that all people can learn and grow in ways that make them more effective in the various leadership roles and processes they take on. Consequent to this, leaders should situate themselves within a mode that values the dignity, worth and contributions of others, that shows respect for people, culture and place, and that delivers the results that the community wants and expects. Leaders need to identify readily that their mandate and activity need to be circumscribed by what is best for their communities, as opposed to being focused in an unseemly fashion on that which will promote their own interests and fuel their ambitions for power, prestige or material gain.

This demands us to display courage. Courage is a quality that shapes a person's character. It is not necessarily a natural disposition, but it is essential in great leadership. This is because leadership inherently effects change in order to obtain some desired future condition that would not otherwise happen. Most people want progress in the first instance as long as they do not have to change very much to get it. It takes courage to expect of people that they need to and can grow in character over time in **Leading for Tomorrow's World**. This inherently means the growth of the whole person in their structured moral agency. It refers to how people live their lives in terms of the fulfilment of their obligations to others, their potential, and their fundamental beliefs about what is good and right for them to do. It is a multi-layered idea that refers to the mark and measure of a person, a notion that encompasses their characteristics and idiosyncrasies, the extent of their resilience and robustness, and their capacity to model and lead through their virtues and qualities.

This process of personal development that improves leader effectiveness is what leadership development is all about. A community needs processes that it follows to identify and nurture leadership. In these, all people should learn about, observe and have an opportunity to practise and refine their leadership skills. When we answer the call to lead, we commit ourselves to enable others to achieve their individual hopes and dreams as well as working together to realise a collective vision. When we lead well, exceptional achievement is possible. And in the end, we need to make sure that we leave an enduring legacy behind, one where we have taught our successors what we know so that excellence and leadership continues.

There is so much for us to learn as leaders. When we fulfil formal roles, we have the opportunity to build teams that have the capacity to do the job together, build the culture that makes the work meaningful and satisfying, and get the job done in the way it should be done. When it is time for us to step out of leadership, we need to be mindful that another will pick up the reins and that our true legacy will be in the service we offered and contributions we made to the lives of others, the cultivation of the places in which we lived and the care we showed for planet of which we were stewards for a short time.

> ### Reflection: Leadership development
>
> Please consider the following questions:
>
> Do I keep myself informed about opportunities to develop my knowledge, skills, disposition and habits as a leader?
>
> Am I a person who takes initiative, shows commitment and seeks to make a contribution?
>
> Do I seek the guidance of mentors to help me reflect on the different aspects of my leadership?
>
> Do I strive to take on roles where I can use my problem-solving and creative thinking to generate new ways of doing things?
>
> Do I model resilience and a positive approach to others in how I lead?

Step Forward and Up
Contribution

Based on everything you have thought about over the course of this chapter, it's time for you to build a plan to Step Forward and Up in your contribution. We are going to use Dr de Bono's Plus, Minus, Interesting process again to help you break down the task of contribution into manageable pieces:

- **Plus** – What's one idea from this chapter that you could make happen in your life tomorrow? What could you do to make this happen? What help will you need? What's a really practical first thing that you could do to make this idea real in your life? What will you do to keep going? How will you know when it's making a difference?
- **Minus** – What's one idea from this chapter that doesn't seem right for you? Why isn't this idea right for you? Is it a case of 'not at all' or 'not yet'? How do you know whether you should hold your ground or shift your thinking on this idea?
- **Interesting** – What's one idea from this chapter that seems like it might be an interesting thing to do but which you're not yet ready to embrace? What might you need to do to ready yourself for this challenge? Who or what might help you to prepare you to take up this challenge in due course? How will you allow the time and space to do this preparation?

Contribution is, in so many ways, related to what you value.

A leader without values is like a ship without a rudder. A leader who acts without reference to their values can bring about hollow results which have lost their fundamental meaning. For example, a team which wins by breaking the rules must deal with the reality that they have cheated. The victory becomes meaningless in the face of the reality that it failed to do the right thing in pursuing the result. Winning at all costs is never really winning.

On the other hand, a leader whose practices are strong and values-based will gain their results with deep satisfaction that what they have done is right, especially when they have persevered through adversity to do this. It is much easier at times to give in to the temptation to cut corners – this is where leaders must step up and insist that those around them do the right thing.

As a leader, you need to adopt strong, positive moral values that align with your team's desired values. You will need to shape the practices of any teams you find yourself in – constantly testing them against the values for which you and others stand. This ensures that your leadership is values-based and that you are being true to yourself through living what is important to you.

Leaders build relationships within teams and help these teams to define their identities. Identity is not that easy to create and define. We construct our individual identities by negotiating the relevance of our values in our daily lives. Some find it easy to live these values, while others struggle to understand and articulate them. If we are less responsible than we would like to be, does that make us less worthy? What about integrity or trustworthiness? How many of us can say that we are always honest? Yet that does not stop us from seeking out the truth that we know will be unfolded for us. It does not stop us from being human.

We believe that whoever influences the core values in a group is the real leader. What might these values be? As I've stated before in this **Character Education Series**, our global research points to the following values as being particularly relevant in **Leading for Tomorrow's World**:

- ✓ Meaning: knowing what is right – leadership 'for good'
- ✓ Transformation: enabling change – leadership 'for change'
- ✓ Authenticity: acknowledging truth – leadership 'for real'
- ✓ Sustainability: nurturing the team and protecting resources – leadership 'for life'
- ✓ Selflessness: serving others first – leadership 'for others'
- ✓ Relationships: encouraging and empowering community – leadership 'for each other'

Leadership is as much about the 'being and becoming' as it is the 'doing' of these values. In the same way, there is a direct relationship between values (the important ideas and concepts that bring meaning to people's lives through their being and becoming) and value (the tangible, material and financial benefits we bring to people's lives through what we do). Great leaders understand this relationship and strive to create a sense of belonging, fulfil potential, and do good and right with a shared and united values and value proposition.

Leaders have a challenging task in this respect. They need to set standards, lead by example and help teams to get things done. They need to develop the character and competencies of others. They need to help us to feel as though we belong and coach us to fulfil our potential. They must model, expect and demand of us that we do good and right things in our lives.

This is the challenge that is presented to you as a leader. You must be able to display the highest standards of personal conduct and integrity at all times. You will, at times, have to stand aside from your peers and put the interests of the team before your own interests. In turn, the opportunity for you to lead in this way will provide opportunities that will support your own personal development.

A leader's ultimate contribution will depend upon their ability to: work as a member of a team; communicate effectively; work hard; serve others; and promote and maintain positive attitudes and behaviours that demonstrate values and value proposition. The success of your leadership can be seen in the collective activity of team members to commit to the unified values and value proposition and accomplish the tasks necessary to get the job done in a manner that is aligned to your desired purpose and culture.

What is it that you might do in your leadership to identify and create a shared values and value proposition through:

- ✓ Disposition towards leadership?
- ✓ Becoming a leader?
- ✓ Formal leadership?
- ✓ Leadership planning and reflection?
- ✓ Leadership development?

What would you need to leave behind to enable you to do this?

Whose help will you need to help you make this happen?

Conclusion
Let's go!

I hope you've gained a lot from this third book of the **Character Education Series** series.

In working through **Leading for Tomorrow's World**, I've shared with you what I've learned about how to connect your purpose to leadership which influences, inspires, directs and motivates others to build a shared vision for the future.

I've also invited you to Step Forward and Up in both chapters to think through your approach to becoming a future-facing leader.

If you have found what we have done together to be valuable, then there is one further book in the series that you might like to consider:

- **Make a Difference** – how to create a plan to put your sense of purpose into practice for the sake of people and place and planet.

If you haven't already, you might also find value in reading the first two books in the series:

- **A Life of Purpose** – how to identify and claim the fundamental reason why for your journey of exploration, discovery and encounter.

- **The Pathway to Excellence** – how to learn, live, lead and work as you strive to become the best version of yourself.

Before we finish, there's one final thought I'd like to share with you.

What kind of leader do you want to become?

During our lives, most of us will take on leadership roles. As this becomes habit, and we build experience in making decisions and following them through as acts of service and contribution, we build the capabilities of our leadership and enact a purpose through this practice that goes beyond our own needs and capacities.

Often, we will show our leadership qualities by supporting the leadership of others and by doing what we do as well as we can as a service for others. Most of us, however, will have some opportunity to exhibit leadership from the front in our lives in formal positions infused with authority to take action and make decisions. We will also lead as parents, as friends, in our work and in our associations. Our context, therefore, shapes our leadership.

We need leaders in our communities who can compel us into a sustainable future without abandoning what we know is truly important. We seek leaders who will understand when to conserve honourable traditions and when to build new traditions by transforming the past into an exciting and achievable future.

Great leadership is about the vision for and unfolding of corporate capability. People of integrity and faith are called to be caretakers of our gifts, and healing agents who seek after justice and truth. If they do this with all sincerity, then they will influence others, leave a powerful legacy and be valued as legitimate leaders of stature. This greatness is always achieved in good company. When a community strives for greatness, it will need all of its members.

We all tend to tire quickly of those who dictate to us how we should fit in, and we admire those who can personalise the collective experience for all of us. We all feel part of something and yet we all wish to be seen as special.

You need to hear and answer a call to lead, to raise your hand and take on responsibility for at least some part of the lives of others. This requires you to have the courage of your convictions. Your call to lead is likely nested within a deep inner desire to strive for greatness for your community. Doubting yourself is a natural part of the process, something to be worked through and used to test the strength of your ideas and potential solutions.

I've seen all over the world how people yearn for authentic leaders who will listen and strive to serve others before themselves. We respond more readily to those who seek to empower the individuality that we want to express and, at the same time, draw us together into a genuine collective effort. We approve of those who can make us feel part of something bigger while at the same time celebrating our distinctiveness.

The funny thing is that we will forgive authentic leadership that is at the same time poorly executed; what we will not tolerate is that which is disingenuous, cynical and self-serving. We will not accept populism when it is revealed to lack the courage of conviction and the commitment of selflessness. We become wary of grand words that are not backed up by results. We look to see how the actions of leaders reveal what sort of person they really are and whether they are worth following. There are any number of ways in which people can project leadership into their surrounds, but unless these are imbued with the will to serve that runs all the way through the leader's being and work, then we are all too often left with hollow words that are self-serving rather than selfless.

Leadership is never simply an individual achievement – it is an opportunity to serve and contribute to individuals, groups and culture. How we think about the nature of our humanity and what we do to augment it through our social structures is just as much a moral matter as it is a practical matter. We should always want our community to be a place that seeks to clear obstacles, and which welcomes all to unfold their gifts and abilities with confidence and a knowledge that they belong and are worthy of our full embrace.

Ultimately, it is in this quest to support others to become the best versions of themselves in pursuit of that which is good and right that we gain a true sense of our potential to lead as part of a community with a common sense of what defines us and drives us on – our values, our mission, our achievements, our culture and our people.

That's the journey of service and contribution in **Leading for Tomorrow's World**.

After all, life is an adventure.

Let's go!

www.ingramcontent.com/pod-product-compliance
Lightning Source LLC
Chambersburg PA
CBHW070336120526
44590CB00017B/2903